Why Not You?

Published by Zaramina Books

ISBN: 978-1-7782921-3-2

Printed. bound, and created in Canada

For my mom & dad...
and every parent who encourages
the pursuit of BIG dreams.

Why Not You?

- Written & Designed by Z.S. Ahmed -

There are those who watch
and there are those who DO.
Have you ever wondered,
which of those are you?

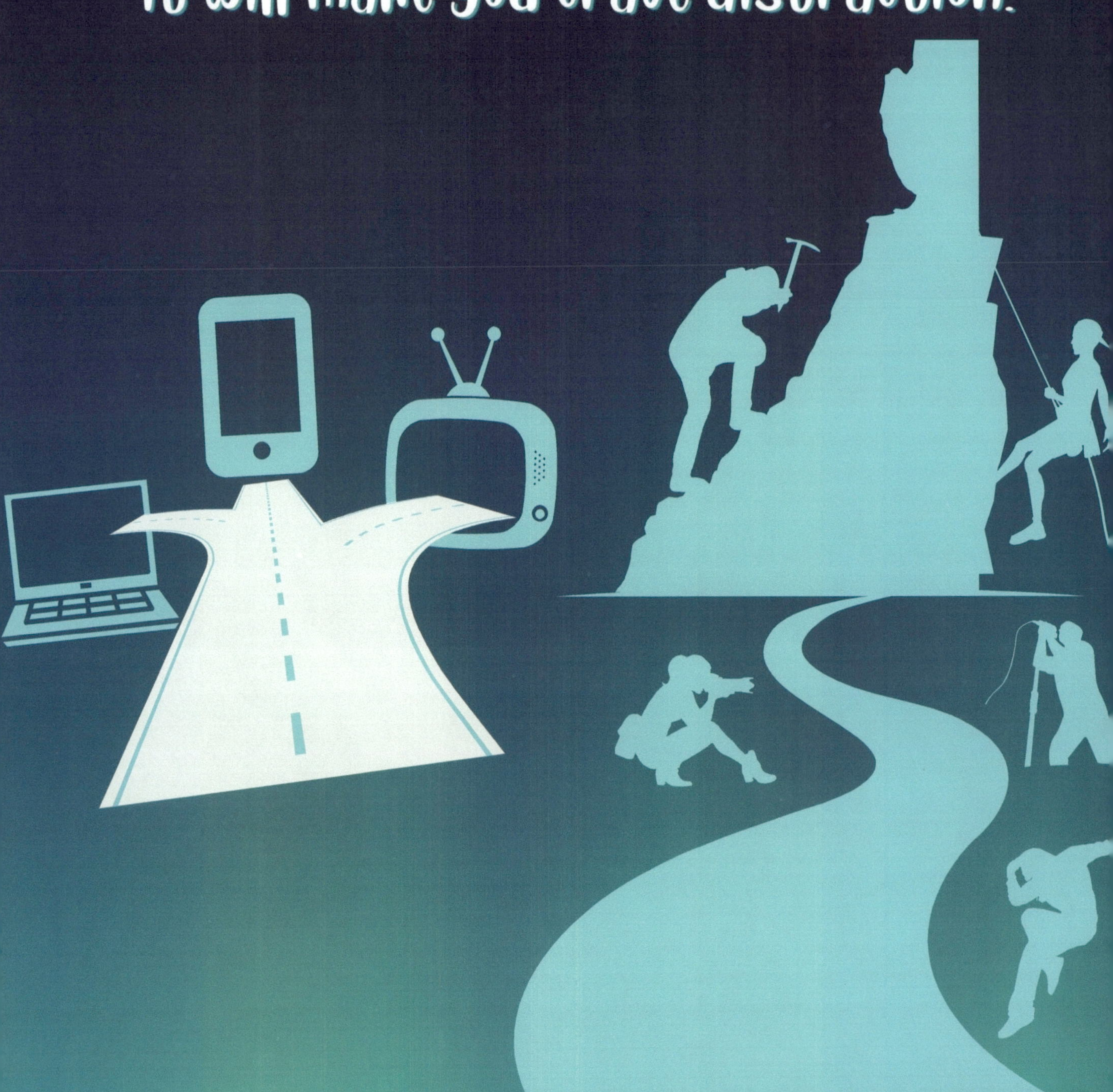

You can take the long and common road;
it will make you crave distraction.
Or you can follow the path of dreams,
and pursue a life of action.

They'll tell you that you're silly
and that you shouldn't try.
"Take the safe and steady road
and kiss that dream good-bye."

"It's a risk that's sure to fail," they'll say,
"You'll end up sad and blue."
But someone has to do great things,
so, tell me...

WHY NOT YOU?

There are ACTORS
and SINGERS...

...there are DANCERS and CHEFS...

...there are ENTREPRENEURS
- and even WRITERS, too...

They caught THEIR dreams
and lightning bolts,
so tell me –

WHY NOT YOU?

Those who do great things
start out like me & you.
They just work so hard each day
and love the things they do.

When you're interested in something
it's easy to put in more time:
like reaching a mountaintop,
and barely recalling the climb.

Parachutes are helpful
and can make us feel less tense,
But using one while on the ground
doesn't seem to make much sense.

You can work 8 hours in a job, each day – that's for sure and true.

But, what if you spent that time, instead, on your 'crazy' dream and YOU?

There are, indeed, two paths in life
and both are hard to follow.
One will pay you for your time,
but may leave you feeling hollow.

This other quiet path feels risky
and includes surprises & strife,
but labors on this golden way
build a more fulfilling life.

So write your dream on Paper
and store it under a Pillow
– or even in a shoe...

...read this poem once each year,
and keep asking...'

Why Not You?

The End?

Write your BIG dreams down here:

(or the things you LOVE to do)

ZARAMINA BOOKS

- Z.S. Ahmed -